HEALING IN HIS Wings

Scribble City PUBLICATIONS

May the goodness of God shine on you like the sun with healing in his wings

Dedication

Prayer changes things, and God hears them. In memory of my parents, especially my mother, Desire A. Joseph, who taught me the importance of prayer, and Walter S. Joseph, my father, for always supporting me through everything.

Acknowledgements

I am grateful to the Holy Spirit, Jesus Christ, my Lord and Saviour, who inspired and guided me in writing this book; and for His direction when writing.
To my adorable husband Kyle, who has never hindered or stopped me from serving God.
Thanks to my son Nathan and my niece Abiane for helping me with the technological and artistic aspects of this book.
I am grateful to Apostle Jenny Watson, co-founder of Kingdom Advance Network, for writing the forward of this book. Despite her busy schedule, she also
supported, encouraged, and guided me through her book coaching programme.

Foreword

"He sent His Word and healed them, And delivered them
from their destructions.
Oh, that men would give thanks to the LORD for His
goodness, And for His wonderful works to
the children of men!" **Psalm 107:20-21**

There have been many books written on the subject of
supernatural or divine healing, and it can be approached
from many different directions. One of the greatest hurdles
for the believer is the question of "what I should do" or "can
do" about it. You see, it is always God's divine will and purpose
to heal people. In fact, that is the very reason Jesus came.

"For this purpose the Son of God was manifested,
that He might destroy the works of the devil."
1 John 3:8

"How God anointed Jesus of Nazareth with the Holy Spirit and with power, who went about doing good and healing all who were oppressed by the devil, for God was with Him."
Acts 10:38

Shauna Chapman has walked this message out with boldness and humility. She is a passionate follower of Yeshua and deeply loves and diligently studies His Word. In this book, she offers significant keys to help anyone step out in faith to believe and receive healing and deliverance from persistent and harassing infirmities and diseases of all kinds.

I personally appreciate how Shauna has stayed true to the Word on this subject, not letting up until a breakthrough comes. I know you will be encouraged in greater revelation and practical consistent steps that will result in manifesting the power and Kingdom of God. Your faith will be increased and your spirit will be nourished by digesting and declaring the absolute truths of God's Word as prescribed herewith.

Apostle Jenny Watson
Co-founder
Kingdom Advance Network
Burton on Trent, UK

Endorsements

Sister Shauna Chapman was inspired to write this "Must Read" book by her personal healing testimony as she encountered miraculous healing from her infirmities that defied all medical therapies, by simply believing and trusting the word of God. She discovered a very easy, non-side effect method of coming out of the bondage of sicknesses and diseases by simply using the Word of God as a healing capsule.

She shares revelations and tips that are very helpful to set someone free from the bondage of infirmities, so that you may live your life in good health. Please don't miss reading this power pact and anointed book. It will help and bless you in Jesus' Name.

Rev. Samuel Amos Kamanga
Gathering of the Unusual Ministries International
Malawi

Shauna Chapman is a dedicated and passionate Woman of God. We've had the pleasure of watching this confident, intelligent, and humble young woman grow in the Lord for over twenty-five years now. *Healing in His Wings* are powerful and anointed words of wisdom, coming straight from her heart.

As an accomplished professional in the medical field, it is very inspiring to see Shauna find balance between the world of medicine and God's Word. We admire her application of the Word in the form of daily capsules. Her book is beneficial, not only for healing from sickness, but for a wholesome life. We are so proud of you for sharing your knowledge and experience, our dear sister in Christ.

Pastor Pauline and Apostle Balgobind Ragnauth
Founders of Lifespring Ministries Cathedral
Guyana
South America.

Contents

SECTION 3
Mental Health Prayers

SECTION 4
Praying for Others

INTRODUCTION

Healing in His Wings was inspired by my own experience. I needed healing even though I knew and understood what the Bible says about healing. I prayed, and I felt like nothing was happening. Can you relate to this? It was a rollercoaster of ups and downs, good days and bad days. As God's child and daughter of Abraham, I was able to sense that something was amiss. I was therefore not ready to accept that. I need to be well again, healed, whole, and able to perform the tasks I used to be able to perform without any issues.

I began to announce, declare, and confess the Word of God (the Holy Scriptures) a few times a day, and before long, the word started to become a part of me. One of the scriptures that touched my spirit, or I could say, I had a light bulb moment, was **Romans 8:11**.

> **Romans 8:11** (NKJV): "But if the Spirit of Him who raised Jesus from the dead dwells in you, He who raised Christ from the dead will also give life to your mortal bodies through His Spirit who dwells in you."

> **Romans 8:11** (AMPC): "And if the Spirit of Him Who raised up Jesus from the dead dwells in you, [then] He Who raised up Christ Jesus from the dead will also restore to life your mortal (short-lived, perishable) bodies through His Spirit Who dwells in you."

> **Romans 8:11** (TPT): "Yes, God raised Jesus to life! And since God's Spirit of Resurrection lives in you, he will also raise your dying body to life with the same Spirit that breathes life into you!"

Another scripture was **1 Peter 2:24** (NKJV): "Who Himself bore our sins in His own body on the tree, that we, having died to sins, might live for righteousness— by whose stripes you were healed."

1 Peter 2:24 (AMP): "He personally carried our sins in His body on the cross, willingly offering Himself on it, as on an altar of sacrifice, so that we might die to sin [becoming immune from the penalty and power of sin] and live for righteousness, for by His wounds you [who believe] have been healed."

It then struck me that Jesus took my sin, pain, and sickness in His body and carried them on the cross. So **why** am I taking and carrying sickness and pain? I asked myself. Jesus took it! I also remembered God telling Moses in the wilderness to make a fiery bronze serpent and set it on a pole, and when the children of Israel looked upon the serpent, they would live. Numbers 21:8. The Lord is more than a bronze serpent; He is the God who loves us, and He is our healer, Yahweh Rapha. *Cast your cares upon the Lord, for He cares.* According to

1 Peter 5:7 (AMP): "Casting all your cares—all your anxieties, all your worries, and all your concerns—once and for all] on Him, for He cares about you [with deepest affection and watches over you very carefully]."

So why am I carrying them all? I don't need to. Neither do you! How amazing is the Word of God!

My mind started to line up with the words written in **Jeremiah 15:16**, "Your words were found, and I ate them. And Your word was to me the joy and rejoicing of my heart. For I am called by your name, O Lord God of Hosts." I was praying, confessing, and declaring it.

I came across a book on healing, and the author had described the consumption of scriptures like eating healing capsules, which bring nourishment and healing to the body. I felt like I was hit by a lightning bolt. What? healing capsules! I stopped, and I felt the Holy Spirit impress upon my heart to write this book, using the Scriptures as healing capsules. And to testify of what taking the healing scriptures like capsules did for me.

Just before the pandemic in 2020, I began to have breathing difficulties. I experienced difficulties going upstairs, riding my bike, walking briskly for 10 to 15 minutes, and climbing up hills or slopes without any obvious cause. The doctors were baffled as to why this was happening. This persisted for a few years. My heartbeat suddenly got irregular at one point, which made the breathlessness worse. The doctor advised I have a cardioversion (a procedure where the heart is stopped and then restarted by shock). The procedure was successful but short-lived; my heart rhythm reverted to the abnormal one. After that, in October 2022, I was taken from work to the hospital and was told I had small blood clots on my brain (called a "brain infract"), which was later determined to be a stroke.

I have no tangible proof of that diagnosis, by God's grace and kindness. My blood pressure even reached previously unheard-of levels, and for months after this, I experienced an unexplained ache in my right leg. The general practitioner also noted that my renal function had suddenly started to decline for no reason.

But I refused to agree with the doctor's report or diagnosis since I believed in God. I wasn't ready to put up with any more discomfort or illness. I am not a sick person, and sickness is not my portion. Things began to change after I went to the Lord and was led to confess the healing Scriptures. The breathlessness abruptly disappeared the day I began writing this book, and I was able to walk upstairs and up hills without any issues. The discomfort subsided. My blood pressure decreased and when I had my kidney tested the last time, the function started to rise once more. God alone is to be praised.

As a qualified registered nurse for many years, I am used to giving and prescribing medication. I would take my medicines without fail, like most people.

So, the aim of this book is to encourage you to adopt the same routine given by doctors and nurses for medication, but instead, to use the Word of God as your healing capsules, tablets, or whatever form of medication. It will need to be used with time intervals. Prescriptions normally indicate how often medication should be taken. For example, once daily, or OD, twice daily, or BD, three times daily, or TDS, and four times daily, or QDS.

PLEASE NOTE: I am not saying to stop taking your medications that your nurse or doctor has prescribed. Kindly keep taking them until you receive the all-clear to stop.

DIVINE HEALTH

"Who forgives all your iniquities, Who heals all
your diseases." **Psalm 103:3**

HEALING GOD'S WAY

This book is to awaken our faith and hearts to receive healing as God intended. By using His written word. Verses 20–22 of Proverbs 4 tell us to, "Pay attention to what I say and bend your ear to what I say." Verses 21 and 22. "Refrain from letting them escape your sight. Hold them close to your heart. For they are health to all their flesh and life to those who find them."

Proverbs 4:20–22 tells us, "My son, give attention to my words; incline your ear to my sayings. Do not let them depart from your eyes; Keep them in the midst of your heart, For they are life to those who find them, and health to all their flesh."

According to **3 John 2,** which says, "Beloved, I pray that you may prosper in all things and be in health, just as your soul prospers," it is God's will that we, his children, be well.

Psalm 103:2-4 offers us all of His benefits, including healing. Verse 3 states, He forgives all your iniquities, He heals all your diseases... not some of your diseases.

Matthew 4:23, "And Jesus went about teaching and proclaim the gospel of the kingdom while curing all manner of illnesses and ailments among the people." In this verse, we can see that healing is what God desires for us to have. Jesus treated all manner of illnesses and ailments, yet most people tend to question God, refuse to accept Him at His word, and deny His ability to heal our bodies. When Jesus was on earth, He spoke these words, "O faithless generation…" **Mark 9:19** and "O you of little faith…" **Matthew 8:26**.

If you are a son or a daughter of God, you have at some point trusted in God to save you. **Ephesians 2:8** states that salvation is a gift from God and that it is obtained by grace—that is, via faith in Jesus Christ and not by human effort.

Thus, the healing Scriptures can be used by us as medication. Most patients take their medications daily in prescribed dosages, and they have faith that the medications will help or cure them. A few of us as God's offspring or believers, also do.

However, God's written Word is living and powerful; it achieves what He purposes and will prosper where it is sent. It never returns to God empty or void.

When Jesus was tempted, He resorted to the Word of God as a weapon against Satan, "saying it is written." In a similar vein, when Satan introduces illness or disease into our bodies, we can and should apply God's word. because Jesus destroyed the devil's works.

1 John 3:8, "He who sins is of the devil, for the devil has sinned from the beginning. For this purpose, the Son of God was manifested, so that He might destroy the works of the devil."

If we are going to allow God to heal us beyond measure. We must receive what Jesus gave his life, and paid a heavy price for. We were healed by His stripes.

1 Peter 2:24, "Who Himself bore our sins in His own body on the tree, that we, having died to sins, might live for righteousness **by whose stripes you were healed**."

Isaiah 53:5, "But He was wounded for our transgressions; He was bruised for our iniquities; the chastisement for our peace was upon Him; and **by His stripes we are healed**."

Some need a change in the way we think. It is up to us to receive; God does not need a cure. And I heard a servant of God, Andrew Wommack once say, and I paraphrase "It's not God who is the giver; rather, it's our receiver that is broken."

Think of it like this: when we plug in a television or radio, that's not when the station is broadcasting; that station is broadcasting around-the-clock; we only receive when we turn on our receiver and tune into it. In the same way. God is constantly revealing Himself; God is constantly revealing love, joy, peace, healing, and salvation; all we require has already been completed and is available to us around-the-clock. We must tune in.

God doesn't need our will to cure us but we must agree with Him for our healing. God has already fulfilled His portion. We don't need to ask God to heal us; we just need to believe what the Bible teaches. God has placed His supernatural power within us. By His wounds, you were healed and restored. Now we can take our authority and speak to the problem about God. Rather than speak to God about the problem.

Say this, "Sickness and disease I command you to leave my life because God has already released His power." He has put it under your control and your command. You can now command and release His power.

> **Isaiah 45:11**, "Concerning the work of My hands, you command Me."

God told us to command Him. Not command Him in the sense that we are the source, but in taking authority together with Him, over the sickness, disease, or problem. It's like electricity; we don't have to call the electric company and ask them to turn on our power; instead, they generate the power and provide it at our request; they won't come to our house and flip the switch; we must give the order and turn the power on. We cannot turn on a light bulb by putting it in our mouths; we are not the source. Although we must give the order for the electricity to be delivered to our home, we are not the source of power.

That is to say, God is the source of our power and has bestowed it upon us; we need only to turn it on by speaking to our issue—in this case, sickness or diseases —and giving commands for things to occur or change in our bodies.

REASONS WHY WE WILL BE HEALED

The Bible makes God's stance on healing very clear throughout the scriptures, and it's important to understand why we will be healed when we seek healing. Here are some reasons why God desires us to be healed:

- The Bible states that nothing is impossible for God, so He is capable of healing us. Using the power that resides within us, He is able to accomplish far more than anything we could possibly ask for or imagine according to Ephesians 3:20. And that strength comes from our confidence in Him— that He can, and will carry out His promises.

- On the cross, Jesus took on our diseases and sicknesses into His own body. And when He passed away, He said it's finished. He did it two thousand years ago. It is not a matter of whether God will accomplish it.

- We do not need to suffer because Jesus did.

- We are Abraham's offspring, or seed. The woman who was bound for eighteen years was identified by Jesus as Abraham's daughter.

- God broke the body of Jesus to ensure healing (**1 Corinthians 11:24**). According to the Bible, we were healed and are cured because of His stripes.

- **Romans 8:1** says that we are not condemned. Therefore, those who are in Christ Jesus and behave in accordance with the Spirit rather than the flesh are no longer subject to condemnation.

- We are new creations, born again. **2 Corinthians 5:17**, "All things have therefore become new; anyone who is in Christ is a new creature; the old things have passed away."

- Our transgressions are covered up and we are pardoned. God chooses to forget our transgressions. He has forgiven us of our sin and has removed it as far as the east is from the west.

- The curse of sin is no longer upon us.

REASONS WHY HEALING MAY BE DELAYED

Although God desires for us to be healed, there are various factors that can delay or hinder healing, and we must address them if we want a manifestation of God's healing promise in our lives.

We must address our unresolved negative feelings and clear any emotional baggage, such as self-loathing, insecurity, regrets, unforgiveness, rejection, shame, fear, anguish, pride, oaths, bitterness, rage, and verbal or unspoken (inner) vows.

Other factors which prevent healing from manifesting are pride, fear, rejection and regret. These are a few examples and we will expound on some of them.

Rejection:

Rejection, especially from parents, can be one of the main sources. Feelings of rejection, if not dealt with give a legal right to the enemy to further lure you into resentment and unforgiveness. Satan looks to find a way for diseases to legally remain within your body. Anything that doesn't have a legal right can't stay in your body for very long.

Proverbs 26:2, "A curse without cause shall not alight." Put another way, a curse cannot remain if there is no reason. As a result, you must let go of all hurt, pain, pride, rejection, and unforgiveness. To free your body and organs from the illness, you must seek to undertake inner healing. Sickness and diseases must go after the inner task is completed since it has no place in your body.

Resentment, Bitterness, and Unforgiveness:

Resentment and bitterness breed unforgiveness, and the Bible teaches us that forgiveness is an essential key in receiving salvation. Repentance is required. You need to repent and move on. According to Mark 11:25, when you pray, forgive. The biggest obstacle to people's healing is unforgiveness.

God knows your heart, therefore, starting with Him is the best course of action. Ask yourself: What stands in my way of my relationship with God? Ask God whether you are offended, angry, or bitter towards Him. Did I break any rules when I was furious and refused to repent? Is there something wrong between us?

Make sure you confess your sins in order to obtain forgiveness, which you can address. Ask the Holy Spirit to reveal any and all areas which may be preventing your healing.

If possible and appropriate, ask your parents. Are you honouring them? Or consider whether you honoured them if they are not alive. If there is any doubt, it must be fixed. If you are unable to bless them, pray for them, think positively about them, let go of any hurt they may have caused you, or give to them, if necessary, your time, money, etc. You have not yet shown forgiveness or fully forgiven them.

To put those hurts behind you, go back and focus on love and positive things. Be the one who refuses to live in bondage due to unforgiveness. Erase the pain and misery, delete the memories, replace them with positive thoughts, and alter your way of thinking.

Gain the ability to forgive and let go of pride, fear, rejection, and unforgiveness.

If you do not deal with and eradicate pride by being willing to forgive or letting go, the illness may still be present in your body. Some people who have died without forgiving never reached their full potential in God.

The majority of the time, the people who cause us pain are actually employed by the devil to prevent us from being where God intends for us to be. **Ephesians 6:12** states that we fight against principalities and powers rather than against flesh and blood. That might just be a spiritual assault.

Oaths and Vows

Things you have said need to be reviewed to remove any negative language. Be careful when speaking, even when listening to music. For instance, some people grab hold of a specific illness or disease and declare it to be their own, saying "my this" or "my that". Saying that is just like agreeing with that disease or sickness. Until you claim it, it is not yours.

Review each and every one of your relationships.

- With God
- With your spouse
- With parents
- With children, step-children
- With siblings
- With grandparents
- With aunts, uncles, cousins, in-laws
- With friends (church family)
- With employer, employees, co workers
- With neighbours
- With acquaintances

You must also forgive yourself for your early year's upbringing. Which might be no fault of yours, and may be due to bloodline issues, care system, schooling, and those in authority, to name a few.

Regrets, bitterness, and fury can cause the bones in your body to dry up. Leading to some bone diseases. Learn to speak right, learn to think right, and pull or cast down wrong imaginations.

I want to encourage you to speak the words of Scripture as you go through this book to begin training your spirit man to receive healing.

RENEWING OUR MIND

Now that we understand the reason for our healing, it is imperative that we renew our thoughts with God's Word. Many Christians commit verses to memory, but do not allow the word to become part of them. **John 1:14** says, "The Word (Jesus) became flesh and dwelt (lived) among us". We therefore must rewire our minds to receive the Word into ourselves; this can be accomplished through meditation. God gave Joshua instructions.

Joshua 1:8, "This Book of the Law shall not depart from your mouth; you shall meditate in it day and night, that you may observe to do according to all that is written in it. For then you will make your way prosperous, and then you will have good success."

Here is one practical way in which we can meditate on the Word of God. Since we are talking about healing, consider a passage from a healing Scripture. After a few times of **saying it aloud**, **personalise it**, and **repeat it.** Ponder, think and muse on it until it becomes part of your being.

Romans 10:17, "So then faith comes by hearing, and hearing by the Word of God." As we read the Word out loud, this begins to build our faith. Also, you can listen to the Word of God. We will be speaking the Word to build our faith in this book.

What is Faith?

According to **Hebrews 11:1,** "Now faith is the substance of things hoped for, the evidence of things not seen." Being healed is a matter of faith—believing in the finished work of our Lord Jesus Christ, and that comes from having our minds renewed with the Word of God. Our mind is a battlefield, and we must win the battle of our minds. This battle is won with the Word of God in our mouths and a heart that believes and trusts in God no matter what the circumstance or situation is around us. This can be difficult. Take a moment to reflect and engage with this process.

This is a simple prayer, speak it out loud:

> *"Father, in the Name of Jesus, give me grace to renew my minds as I ponder Your word. Let your Word become a part of me. Let it bring light into every area of my body. Amen."*

Instead of the unfavourable report from the doctors, we must be prepared to trust the report of the Lord. The report of the Lord is what He says in His Word. For instance, in the last portion of **Joel 3:10**, He says, "Let the weak **say** I am strong."

We are going to reprogramme our minds so we can win the battle for our healing with scriptural weapons, for He has given us the sword of the Spirit, which is the Word of God. We are going to accomplish this by reprogramming our subconscious minds. Both the conscious and subconscious minds exist.

The Oxford Dictionary explains it this way: The mind is "The element of a person that enables them to be aware of the world and their experiences, to think and to feel, the faculty of consciousness and thoughts."

Everything you are aware of and thinking about is called the conscious mind.

As the Cambridge Dictionary defines it. The portion of your mind that retains knowledge when you are not consciously striving to remember it is called the subconscious mind, and it has an unconscious influence on our actions.

We need to conduct constructive dialogues, or in other words, positive conversations with ourselves, in order to leave the conscious mind and enter the sub-conscious mind.

Consider the Scripture you are meditating on for healing at the moment. In this instance, **Jeremiah 30:17a** will be applied. The Lord declares, "For I will restore health to you and heal you of your wounds, says the Lord."

Let's say you read this verse aloud several times, make it special or personal for yourself, and then you could say, for instance, *"Yes, Lord, You will heal my wounds and restore my health, because this is what You said in Your word."* By doing this, you are forcing the negative feeling or report that says, "I'm sick, and the doctor's report says this and that," or "I don't feel well today," to be pushed out of your conscious mind.

To enter the sub-conscious mind so that it's not a belief but "a knowing"(I know, that I know, that I know); the knowing is faith. I know He has restored my health and healed my wounds. God will restore and heal you. You will be in a better position to receive your healing; you just flip the switch. The light came on.

Do this several times a day as a practice. Begin each day for a little while, then work your way up to at least thirty minutes or an hour each morning and evening. You can begin with one Scripture and continue adding more as you see fit. It requires effort, devotion, consistency and diligence, as well as intentionality.

Just as we take the medications or tablets that our doctors

or nurses prescribe. God is the greatest physician, and He sends His Word to heal us. His word is like medicine which gives life.

At the time of writing this book, we are in the year 2024, the Hebrew year 5784 and the *pey* decade, which is the decade of the mouth. The word pey is pictured as a mouth, which is the number eighty (80), hence, the decade of the mouth. It's no better time to practice this. Speaking out loud, reading the Word out loud, and then having that conversation out loud. When I say loud, it's not for you to disturb others, but so that you are able to hear yourself speaking. Faith comes by hearing, and hearing by the Word of God.

I hope this arouses your faith in order for you to get healed.

We are going to be declaring, decreeing, confessing and praying God's Word for the rest of this book. For those who are unfamiliar with this, here is a brief explanation.

A declaration is a formal, explicit statement or proclamation.

Declaring something entails saying it in a solemn (formal, dignified, serious) and forceful (clear) way. An official decree is a legally binding order.

HEALED AND WHOLE

What does the term "healed" mean? Healed is the past tense and past participle of the word heal, according to the Oxford dictionary. "Restore the soundness or health" of a wound, injury, or person. To recover your health or soundness.

When something is damaged, out of order, out of harmony, or dysfunctional, it needs healing or fixing. When we are out of order in our bodies due to diseases, sicknesses, or infirmities, then we need fixing! Agreed?

The Oxford Dictionary defines "whole" as "an adjective that means "all of or "entire." Alternatively, intact in a single piece.

Also, a noun means a thing that is complete in itself or all of something.

The state of creating a whole or unity, that is harmonious and complete is known as wholeness, or the condition of not being harmed or broken.

Luke chapter 17:11–19 provides an extremely fascinating account of how Jesus healed the ten lepers. Due to their distance from Jesus and the leprosy, these men raised their voices and begged for forgiveness and mercy.

"'Jesus then said to them, "Go show yourselves to the priest." They went, but on their way to the priest, something happened: they were cleansed. But one of them, when he saw he was healed (the skin was not broken), went back to glorify God and give thanks to Jesus. Then Jesus said, "Were there not ten cleansed?"'(NKJV).

Some translations say, "Were there not ten healed?"

Jesus then said to the man, "Arise, go your way. Your faith has made you well or whole."(TPT).

The amplified version Bible says "God has restored you to health".

Have you ever considered why Jesus said, "You are whole and well because of your faith?"

You see, we can be healed, completely well, undamaged, fully restored, and able to function in every way. Jesus died so that we can be complete. He desires for us to be whole. For us to live long, healthy lives, He destroyed the devil's works. What a blessing and honour it is to be a citizen of God's kingdom! Well, that's a whole different story, God's citizen.

RECEIVING SALVATION

You might not know Jesus at all, be an agnostic (non-believer), or have never heard the good news of Jesus' miraculous power to save and heal. You may not be walking with God for whatever reason, but you may be in need or desire to be made well and whole. You must be reborn (accept Jesus now), as seen in **John 3:3,** "Jesus replied, "I tell you the truth, unless you are born again, you cannot see the Kingdom of God." Although God is sovereign, sometimes He will heal someone who is not a believer just to show his love, mercy, and compassion. We can see in John 5:1-15 where Jesus healed the man at the pool of Bethesda. Then, in verse 14, He told the man not to continue to sin. In other words, walk away from a sinful lifestyle.

The only path to the Father is through Jesus.

Jesus declared, "I am the way, the truth, and the life," in **John 14:6.** I am the only path that leads to the Father.

> **Romans 10:9–10,** "That if you confess with your mouth the Lord Jesus and believe in your heart that God has raised Him from the dead, you will be saved. For with the heart one believes unto righteousness, and with the mouth confession is made unto salvation."

Don't believe that because of who you are or what you have done, Jesus will not accept you, that you are too far gone, or that you are unworthy.

> **John 3:16,** "God so loved the world that He gave His only begotten Son, that whoever believes in Him should not perish but have everlasting life."

And 2 Peter 3:9 demonstrates God's deep love for us all. The Lord is longsuffering toward us and wants everyone to known Him as Father and Healer.

2 Peter 3:9 (NKJV): "The Lord is not slack concerning His promise, as some count slackness, but is longsuffering toward us, not willing that any should perish but that all should come to repentance."

I'm encouraged by **2 Peter 3:8–9** (MSG):

"Don't overlook the obvious here, friends. With God, one day is as good as a thousand years, a thousand years as a day. God isn't as late with his promise as some measure of lateness. He is restraining himself on account of you, holding back the end because he doesn't want anyone to be lost. He's giving everyone space and time to change."

According to The Passion translation (TPT), **2 Peter 3:9,**

"This means that, contrary to man's perspective, the Lord is not late with his promise to return, despite some measure of lateness. But rather, his "delay" simply reveals his loving patience towards you, because he does not want any to perish but all to come to repentance."

If you have decided or are wondering how you can partake of this promise and enter the Kingdom of God, the Father, here is what you need to know and do.

To become part of the family of God and to know God personally, you must be born again. These simple steps will help in the process.

A. Accept that you need a Saviour. You can't please God in yourself or pay the sure penalty for missing His mark of perfection, which is sin. Everyone has sinned. Accept this fact. Accept that He is the only one who can help.

B. Believe that Jesus and only Jesus, is the perfect sacrifice for sin. He really lived, it is a proven fact, and died, and was raised up to eternal life and lives by His Spirit within those who repent (confess their sins and turn away from the lifestyle of sin, accepting His free gift of eternal life).

C. Confess—in two ways. Firstly, confess your sinful state and need of a Saviour. Ask Jesus for forgiveness and receive His forgiveness. Secondly, confess, **"Jesus is my Lord and Saviour."** Tell someone!

This simple prayer sums all this up for you. Pray, believe, and somethings will happen!!

Speak this prayer aloud. The words of the late Billy Graham.

> *"Dear heavenly Father, I know that I am a sinner, and I ask for your forgiveness. I believe that Jesus Christ died for my sins and rose from the dead. I turn from my sins. I invite you to come into my heart and life. I want to trust and follow you as my Lord and Saviour." In Jesus name. Amen.*

Welcome to the family of God. This is your new birth, or as some would say, you are now born again. Love Jesus with all of your heart and live for Him. Every day, seek him out, pray, and read the word (the Bible). I love you, but Jesus loves you more. Bless you.

—— Section 2 ——

HEALING CAPSULES

The Word of God

"Your words were found, and I ate them, And Your word was to me the joy and rejoicing of my heart; For I am called by Your name, O LORD God of hosts". **Jeremiah 15:16**

How it Works

Just as you would take regular medication, select any out of the four daily capsule prayers and declarations (that is once, twice, three or four times) as you desire. Read it aloud, pray and declare daily. Remain consistent, persistent, and committed until the manifestation of your healing.

ONCE DAILY (OD) PRAYER

Use once daily anytime of the day

Begin with a time of praise, worship, adoration, and thanksgiving to God.

Psalms 100:1-5, "Make a joyful shout to the LORD, all you lands! Serve the LORD with gladness; Come before His presence with singing. Know that the LORD, He is God; It is He who has made us, and not we ourselves; We are His people and the sheep of His pasture. Enter into His gates with thanksgiving, And into His courts with praise. Be thankful to Him, and bless His name. For the LORD is good."

Confessions

Make these confessions out loud (speak out so that you can hear yourself).

Malachi 4:2, "But to you who fear My name, the Sun of Righteousness shall arise with healing in His wings, and you shall go out and grow fat like stall-fed calves."

Exodus 15:26 and said, "If you diligently heed the voice of the Lord your God and do what is right in His sight, give ear to His commandments, and keep all His statutes, I will put none of the diseases on you that I have brought on the Egyptians. For I am the Lord who heals you."

Psalms 30:2, "O Lord my God, I cried out to You, and You healed me."

Psalms 103:3, "Who forgives all your iniquities, who heals all your diseases."

Isaiah 53:4, " Surely, He has borne our griefs and carried our sorrows, yet we esteemed Him stricken, smitten by God, and afflicted."

Isaiah 53:5, "But He was wounded for our transgressions; He was bruised for our iniquities; the chastisement for our peace was upon Him; and by His stripes we are healed."

Romans 8:11, "But if the Spirit of Him who raised Jesus from the dead dwells in you, He who raised Christ from the dead will also give life to your mortal bodies through His Spirit who dwells in you."

Romans 8:11 (AMPC): "And if the Spirit of Him Who raised up Jesus from the dead dwells in you, then He Who raised up Christ Jesus from the dead will also restore to life your mortal (short-lived, perishable) bodies through His Spirit Who dwells in you."

Romans 8:11(TPT): "Yes, God raised Jesus to life! And since God's Spirit of Resurrection lives in you, he will also raise your dying body to life with the same Spirit that breathes life into you!"

John 8:36, "Therefore, if the Son makes you free, you will indeed be free."

Romans 8:2, "For the law of the Spirit of life in Christ Jesus has made me free from the law of sin and death."

Romans 8:32, "He who did not spare His own Son but delivered Him up for us all, how shall He not with Him also freely give us all things?"

Psalms 138:7, "Though I walk in the midst of trouble, You will revive me; You will stretch out Your hand against the wrath of my enemies; and Your right hand will save me."

Psalms 138:8, "The Lord will perfect that which concerns me. Your mercy, O Lord, endures forever. Do not forsake the works of Your hands."

Psalms 143:11, "Revive me, O Lord, for Your name's sake! For your righteousness' sake, bring my soul out of trouble."

Psalms 143:11 (AMPC): "Save my life, O Lord, for Your name's sake; in Your righteousness, bring my life out of trouble and free me from distress."

1 Peter 2:24, "Who Himself bore our sins in His own body on the tree, that we, having died to sins, might live for righteousness by whose stripes you were healed."

Proverbs 3:5-8, "Trust in the Lord with all your heart, and lean not on your own understanding. In all your ways, acknowledge Him, and He shall direct your paths. Do not be wise in your own eyes; fear the Lord and depart from evil. It will be good for your flesh and strong for your bones."

Ezekiel 16:6, "And when I passed by you and saw you struggling in your own blood, I said to you in your blood, 'Live!' Yes, I said to you in your blood, 'Live!'

Joel 3:21, "For I will acquit them of the guilt of bloodshed, whom I had not acquitted, for the Lord dwells in Zion."

Joel 3:21 (KJV): "For I will cleanse their blood that I have not cleansed, for the Lord dwelleth in Zion."

1 Corinthians 3:16, "Do you not know that you are the temple of God and that the Spirit of God dwells in you?"

Proverbs 4:20-22, "My son, give attention to my words. Incline your ear to my sayings. Do not let them depart from your eyes; keep them in the midst of your heart; For they are life to those who find them, and health to all their flesh."

2 Timothy 1:7, "God has not given us a spirit of fear but of power, love, and a sound mind."

Matthew 15:13, "'But He answered and said, "Every plant which My heavenly Father has not planted will be uprooted."'"

Mark 11:23-24, "For assuredly, I say to you, whoever says to this mountain, 'Be removed and be cast into the sea,' and does not doubt in his heart but believes that those things he says will be done, he will have whatever he says. Therefore, I say to you, whatever things you ask when you pray, believe that you will receive them, and you will have them.

3 John 1:2, "Beloved, I pray that you may prosper in all things and be in good health, just as your soul prospers."

Psalms 34:19, "Many are the afflictions of the righteous, but the Lord delivers him out of them all."

John 10:10, "The thief does not come except to steal, to kill, and to destroy. I have come that they may have life and that they may have it more abundantly."

- Father, in the Name of Jesus, I thank You for Your mighty power to heal all sickness.

- Thank you, God, for You are the God that heals, and thank you for healing me.

- I release the light and life of God into my body to remove all pain, disease, and anything that should not be there (growths, tumours). See yourself in union with God, and receiving His life-giving flow into your body.

- The same Spirit that raised Jesus from the dead lives on the inside of me and is quickening my mortal body, all my cells, my organs, my brain, my nerves, my blood, all my limbs, my eyes, my ears, my skin, and my bones.

- I command every disease (mention the specific disease...) in my blood and body organs to die now, in Jesus' Name.

- Let my blood and body reject every foreign evil entity, everything, and anything planted in my body that is not of God. Be uprooted and come out now. In Jesus Name.

- Let the blood of Jesus speak disappearance to every infirmity in my life.

- Holy Spirit, speak deliverance and healing into my life in Jesus's Name.

- I apply the blood of Jesus to you spirit of infirmity. And command you to flee now.

- O Lord, let Your healing hand be stretched out upon my life now.

- O Lord, let Your deliverance hand be stretched out upon my life now.

- O Lord, let Your miracle hand be stretched out upon my life now.

- I cancel and disannul every engagement with the spirit of death, in the Name of Jesus.

- I receive and accept the abundant life that You came to give me, Lord.

- I rebuke every form of sickness, disease, and pain in or on my body. And I command you to leave now. In Jesus Name.

- I destroy the grip and operation of sickness upon my life, in the Name of Jesus.

- O Lord, let my negativity be converted to positivity. I decree and declare that I am healed; sickness and disease are far from me.

- Father, let the whirlwind of God scatter every vessel of infirmity fashioned against my life, in the Name of Jesus.

- I shall see sickness no more in my body or life. In Jesus Name.

- I command death upon all sickness in any area of my life, in Jesus's Name.

- Let every fountain of discomfort in my life dry up now, in the Name of Jesus.

- For every internal disorder, receive order now. In the Name of Jesus.

- Let every organ in my body function the way

HEALING IN HIS WINGS

God created you to function.

- I speak to every dead organ in my body. Receive life now. Live! Hear the word of the Lord and be made whole. In the Name of Jesus.

- Father, Lord, let every agent of sickness working against my health disappear now, in Jesus' Name.

- Father, Lord, let every germ of infirmity in my body die, in Jesus' Name.

- I release my body from every curse of infirmity in Jesus' Name.

- I withdraw every conscious and unconscious cooperation with sickness, in the Name of Jesus.

- Father, let the blood of Jesus flush every evil deposit out of my blood.

- I recover every organ of my body from every evil altar. In the Name of Jesus.

- Thank you, God, for your healing. Amen and amen.

TWICE DAILY (BD) PRAYERS

Use two times a day, at 6 am and 6 pm

Begin with a time of praise, worship, adoration, and thanksgiving to God.

Psalms 100:1-5, "Make a joyful shout to the LORD, all you lands! Serve the LORD with gladness; Come before His presence with singing. Know that the LORD, He is God; It is He who has made us, and not we ourselves; We are His people and the sheep of His pasture. Enter into His gates with thanksgiving, And into His courts with praise. Be thankful to Him, and bless His name. For the LORD is good."

Confessions

Make these confessions out loud (speak out so you can hear yourself).

You can use both together and/or separately.

ONE

Father, You are great, and You perform wonderful deeds. You alone are God. How great are Your signs, and how powerful are Your wonders? Lord, You are high above all the nations. Your glory is higher than the heavens. Who can be compared with You, our God, who is enthroned on high? We give thanks because You are near. People everywhere will tell of your wonderful deeds. Lord, I thank you for salvation, the greatest miracle of all. Thank You for Your eternal and unconditional love and unmerited grace. Thank You for sending Your Son, Jesus, to destroy the works of the devil and bring us hope, health, and healing. Lord, You are good, and your mercy endures forever.

I believe Jesus Christ is the same yesterday, today, and forever. Heavenly Father, You brought Israel out of Egypt with signs and wonders and with a strong hand and powerful arm. Jesus Christ, Your Son, cleansed lepers, healed the sick, raised the dead, and did many other things in the presence of His disciples. Therefore, Father, I expect You to display your glory in my life, heal me, and deliver me. With You, nothing is impossible. I expect sickness and diseases to leave now, and my mind and soul to be set free. I confess that Your healing power will operate through me. Help me to trust in You with all my heart, and do not depend on my own understanding. Thank You, Lord, for perfecting everything that concerns me and revive me for Your Name's sake.

Father, forgive me for doubting Your word and Your works. Forgive me for acting religious, putting on a form of godliness, and rejecting and denying Your power to perform healings, signs, and wonders in my life. Lord, please forgive me and restore the joy of my salvation. Holy Spirit remind me of anyone I need to forgive and help me to forgive them quickly.

Lead me not into temptation but deliver me from the evil one.

Father, You are the Almighty! Only You can open the eyes of the blind and unplug the ears of the deaf. You cause the lame to leap like deer and those who cannot speak to sing for joy. You cause springs to gush forth in the wilderness and streams to water the wasteland.

You cause the parched ground to become a pool, and You create springs of water to satisfy the thirsty land. Great and awesome is Your Name.
in Jesus' name.
Amen.

The above prayer is complied using the pattern of the Lord's Prayer, or the Model Prayer in **Mathew 6:9-13.**

Scriptural Readings:

Psalms 86:10, Daniel 4:3, Psalms 113:4-5, Psalms 75:1, Psalms 136:1, 1 John 3:8, Hebrews 13:8, Psalms 136:11-12, Luke 7:22, John 20:30, Luke 1:37, Proverbs 3:5, Psalms 138:8, 2 Timothy3:5, Psalms 91:12, Matthew 15:13, and Isaiah 35:5-7

Two

Heavenly Father, In the name of Jesus, I thank You for your promises of health and healing. Your word is certain, and You are always true.
I declare that I am a child of God through faith in Jesus Christ and Abraham's seed and heir, according to promise.

Lord, I put You in remembrance of Your Word. You said that as I serve You. You will bless my bread and water and take sickness away from me, and no one will suffer miscarriage or be barren, and you will cause me to fulfil my days. Also, You will take away all sickness and afflict me with none of the terrible diseases I read and hear about in the world, which represent Egypt, for You are the Lord who heals.

It is God's will for me to be healed, and it is His will that I prosper and be in health even as my soul prospers. Jesus carried my sickness, disease, and pain on the cross; therefore, I do not have to carry them. By His stripes, I am healed. So, I speak healing and life over my body. His Word says death and life are in the power of my tongue. I declare that the same Spirit that raised Jesus from the dead lives on the inside of me and is quickening, giving life to my mortal body.

Jesus was revealed to destroy the works of the devil. I bind and command every demonic spirit of sickness, pain, or infirmity to leave my body now by the authority of the Name of Jesus, and I curse the roots of any stubborn disease and command you to die now. In the Name of Jesus.

Revive, me O Lord, for Your name's sake! For your righteousness' sake, bring my life out of trouble. The Lord will perfect that which concerns me. Your mercy, O Lord, endures forever; do not forsake the works of Your hands.

My body is the temple of the Holy Spirit, and all of God's fullness dwells in me. I will glorify Him with my body, which belongs to Him. Lord, I thank You for Your Word. I ate them, and Your words became a joy to me and the delight of my heart. A joyful, cheerful heart brings healing to the body and soul.

I will not forget Your benefits of forgiveness, despite all I've done. You've healed me inside and out from every disease.

I decree and declare that my body is completely healed, restored, and made whole to fulfil God's will, plans, and purpose for my life.
In Jesus mighty Name.
Amen.

Scriptural Readings:

Galatians 3:26, Exodus 23:25-26, Deuteronomy 7:26, Exodus 15:26, 3 John 2:5, 1 Peter 2:24, 1 John 3:8, Proverbs 18:21, Romans 8:11, Psalms 143:11, Psalms 138:8, 1 Corinthians 6:19, Colossians 2:19, 1 Corinthians 6:20, Jeremiah 15:16, Proverbs 17:22 (TPT), Psalms 103:3 (TPT), Jeremiah 29:11

THREE TIMES DAILY (TDS) PRAYERS

Use three times a day: 6 am, 2 pm and 10 pm

Begin with a time of praise, worship, adoration, and thanksgiving to God.

Psalms 100:1-5, "Make a joyful shout to the LORD, all you lands! Serve the LORD with gladness; Come before His presence with singing. Know that the LORD, He is God; It is He who has made us, and not we ourselves; We are His people and the sheep of His pasture. Enter into His gates with thanksgiving, And into His courts with praise."

Confessions

Make these confessions out loud (speak out so you can hear yourself).

You can also pray these prayers using the OD and BD prayers, either in addition to these prayers, or separately, praying three times daily.

Isaiah 53:5, "But He was wounded for our transgressions; He was bruised for our iniquities; the chastisement for our peace was upon Him; and by His stripes we are healed."

- Let praise and glory be to God and Father of our Lord Jesus, who has already lavished upon me as a love gift every spiritual and physical blessing, all because he sees me wrapped in Christ. This is why I celebrate Him with all my heart.

- Confession brings about possession; now I receive the healing promises of God in my life, and I ask my Father in heaven to command them to begin to be operational in my spirit, soul, and body.

- Lord, heal me of every soul wound that may

have contributed to any sickness in my body.

- I confess my faith in God, the Father of Jesus. Jesus Christ is the Word of God sent into the world to heal me. I confess my faith in the Word of God. The Word of God is my healing capsule, and as I take it now, it will minister destruction to any inherited or demonic infirmity, sickness, or disease in my body. It will minister health to my body and glory and honour to God, my Healer.

- It is written, I shall worship the Lord my God, and He will bless my bread and water and take sickness away from among me. Let this Scripture come true in my life right now.

- It is written that when I am sick, lying upon my bed of suffering, God will restore me. He will raise me up again and restore me back to health. So, in my sickness, I say, "Lord, be my kind Healer. Heal my body and soul; heal me, God! I have confessed my sins to you. I swallow these promises of God in faith.

- Surely, He shall deliver me from the snare of the fowler and from the noisome pestilence. No evil shall befall me, nor shall any plague come near my dwelling. The Lord has forgiven all my iniquities; He has healed all my diseases. He has redeemed my life from destruction. He has crowned me with loving kindness and satisfied my mouth with good things so much that my youth is renewed like the eagle's. I ask these Scriptures to renew my body right now, and I receive it in faith.

- Lord, You sustain the weak and feeble and lift up those who are bent over with burdens of shame. You open the eyes of the blind and fully restore those bent over with shame. You love those who love and honour you. He heals the wounds of every shattered heart. Let the Spirit of God in these scriptures quicken my spirit, soul, and body.

- It is written, my son; attend to my words; incline thine ears unto my sayings. Let them not depart from thine eyes; keep them in the midst of thine heart. For they are life to those that find them, and health to all their flesh. For by Me thy days shall be multiplied, and the years of thy life shall be increased. A tender, tranquil heart will make me healthy, but jealousy can make me sick. Nothing is more appealing than speaking beautiful, life-giving words. For they release sweetness to my soul and inner healing to my spirits. Jeremiah said, "Your words were found by me, and I did eat them, and they are joy and rejoicing in my heart." I eat all the healing capsules in the above Scriptures of God, and they shall bring healing and refreshing to my flesh and bones.

- He gives power to the weak, and to those who have no might, He increases strength. For I will restore health to you and heal you of your wounds, says the Lord. Behold, I will bring it health and healing; I will heal them and reveal to them the abundance of peace and truth. For I will cleanse their blood that I have not cleansed, for the Lord dwelleth in Zion. I am a child of promise, and I stand on the covenant promise of God for me. I receive every benefit of divine health made to me through those words of God.

- It is written that Jesus himself took away all my infirmities and bore all my sickness on the cross of Calvary. He bore all my grief and carried my sorrows. He was stricken, smitten, afflicted, and wounded so that I might be saved. He was bruised for my iniquities, and the chastisement of my peace was upon Him, and by His stripes I am healed. The Bible says, when I see this, my head shall rejoice, and my bones shall flourish like grass; the Hand of the Lord shall be known to me, and His indignation to my enemies.

- Through the death and resurrection of Jesus, the works of the devil, who had the power of death, sickness, and disease, were destroyed. Therefore, because Jesus Christ has redeemed me from this curse and came to give me abundant life, you demons of infirmities and sickness, you have no more dominion over my body. I have confessed my sins, which I have committed against my Lord, and it is written that if we freely admit that we have sinned and confess our sins, He is faithful and just and will forgive our sins and cleanse us continually from all unrighteousness. He himself said he would be merciful and gracious towards my unrighteousness, my wickedness, my sins, and my lawless deeds and would remember them no more. Therefore, let everything that the accuser is holding against me in order to keep afflicting me be removed by the blood of Jesus.

- Heal me, O Lord, and I shall be healed; save me, and I shall be saved, for You are my praise. Let Your thoughts that are not of evil towards me begin to prosper in my life. You wish me above all things that I may prosper and be in good health, even as my soul prospers. I receive this prosperity. God has not given me the spirit of fear but of power, love, and a sound mind. I stand against the devil with the blood of Jesus, and I bind any further attacks and afflictions.

- The Lord is my strength and power, and He makes my way perfect. The Lord is my salvation; He is my deliverer, redeemer, and protector. The joy of the Lord is my strength. No longer shall I be weak and become feeble again. I have eaten the flesh of Jesus and drunk His blood. I declare I shall not die but live to tell the world what the Lord has done for me, who loves me, died for me, and washed me in His own blood.

- The Lord will guide me continually, satisfy my soul in drought, and strengthen my bones; I shall be like a well-watered garden and like a spring of water, whose waters do not fail.

- Now, I am God's workmanship, created in

Christ Jesus for good works. And I will praise you, Lord, for I am fearfully and wonderfully made. Marvellous are Your works, and my soul knows very well. I am one with Christ. I declare that sickness has no place in me anymore. I have an abundant life. Jesus has restored to me all that the devil has stolen, killed, and destroyed. No longer can any negative confession I made in the past about my health prosper. God has started new things in my spirit, soul, and body, and they have already begun to spring up. Amen.

Scriptural Readings:

Ephesians 1:3 (TPT), Psalm 107:20 (TPT), Proverbs 3:8, Exodus 23:25, Psalm 41:3-4 (TPT), Psalm 91:3 & 10 (TPT), Psalm 103:3-5, Psalm 145:14, 146:8, 147:3 (TPT), Proverbs 9:11, Proverbs 14:30 (TPT), Proverbs 10:24 (TPT), Jeremiah 15:16, Isaiah 40:29, Jeremiah 30:17, 33:6, Joel 3:21, 1 Peter 2:24, Isaiah 53:4-5, 66:14, Galatians 3:13, John 10:10, 1 John 1:9 (AMP), Hebrews 8:12, Jeremiah 17:14, 3 John 2, 2 Timothy 1:7, 2 Samuel 22:33, Nehemiah 8:10, Hebrews 12:12, John 6:53, Psalm 118:17 (TPT), Isaiah 58:11 and John 17:21

FOUR TIMES DAILY (QDS) PRAYERS

Use it four times a day: 6 am, Noon, 6 pm and Midnight

Begin with a time of praise, worship, adoration, and thanksgiving to God.

Psalms 100:1-5, "Make a joyful shout to the LORD, all you lands! Serve the LORD with gladness; Come before His presence with singing. Know that the LORD, He is God; It is He who has made us, and not we ourselves; We are His people and the sheep of His pasture. Enter into His gates with thanksgiving, And into His courts with praise. Be thankful to Him, and bless His name. For the LORD is good."

Confessions

Make these confessions out loud (speak out so you can hear yourself).

You can pray the prayers used in OD, BD and TDS in combination or separately to pray four times daily.

— Section 3 —

MENTAL HEALTH

"You will keep him in perfect peace. Whose mind is stayed on You, Because he trusts in You." **Isaiah 26:3**

PRAYER DECLARATION FOR THE MIND

Mental Health: What is it?

Our emotional, psychological, and social well-being are all part of our mental health. It influences our feelings, thoughts, and behaviours. It also influences how we respond to stress, interact with people, and make wise decisions. Every stage of life, from infancy and adolescence to adulthood, is critical for mental health.

Why is Mental Well-being Critical to General Health?

Both physical and mental well-being are crucial aspects of total health. Depression, for instance, raises the risk of a variety of physical health issues, especially chronic illnesses like diabetes, heart disease, and stroke. In a similar vein, having long-term medical issues can raise your chance of developing a mental illness.

Prayer and Declarations for the Mind

Begin with a time of praise, worship, adoration, and thanksgiving to God.

Psalms 100:1-5, "Make a joyful shout to the LORD, all you lands! Serve the LORD with gladness; Come before His presence with singing. Know that the LORD, He is God; It is He who has made us, and not we ourselves; We are His people and the sheep of His pasture. Enter into His gates with thanksgiving, And into His courts with praise. Be thankful to Him, and bless His name. For the LORD is good"

Confessions

Confess the Word of God over your mind. Make these confessions out loud (speak out so you can hear yourself).

- **Isaiah 26:3,** "You will keep him in perfect peace. Whose mind is stayed on You, Because he trusts in You."

- **1 Peter 5:7,** "Casting all your care upon Him, for He cares for you."

- **Philippians 4:6-7,** "Be anxious for nothing, but in everything, by prayer and supplication, with thanksgiving, let your requests be made known to God, and the peace of God, which surpasses all understanding, will guard your hearts and minds through Christ Jesus."

- **Luke 12:29,** "And do not seek what you should eat or what you should drink, nor have an anxious mind."

- **1 Corinthians 2:16,** "For who has known the mind of the Lord that he may instruct Him? But we have the mind of Christ."

- **Philippians 2:5,** "Let this mind be in you, which was also in Christ Jesus."

- **1 Thessalonians 4:11,** "That you also aspire to lead a quiet life, to mind your own business, and to work with your own hands, as we commanded you."

- **2 Timothy 1:7,** "For God has not given us

a spirit of fear, but of power and of love and of a sound mind."

- **Matthew 22:37,** Jesus said to him, "'You shall love the Lord your God with all your heart, with all your soul, and with all your mind."

- **Romans 12:2,** "And do not be conformed to this world, but be transformed by the renewing of your mind, that you may prove what is that good and acceptable and perfect will of God."

- **Colossians 3:2,** "Set your mind on things above, not on things on the earth."

- **2 Corinthians 10:5,** "Casting down arguments and every high thing that exalts itself against the knowledge of God, bringing every thought into captivity to the obedience of Christ."

- **2 Corinthians 10:5** (AMPC): "[Inasmuch as we] refute arguments and theories and reasonings and every proud and lofty thing that sets itself up against the [true] knowledge of God; and we lead every thought and purpose away captive into the obedience of Christ (the Messiah, the Anointed One)."

- **Titus 3:5,** "Not by works of righteousness which we have done, but according to His mercy He saved us, through the washing of regeneration and renewing of the Holy Spirit."

- **Philippians 4:8,** "Finally, brethren, whatever things are true, whatever things are noble, whatever things are just, whatever things are pure, whatever things are lovely, whatever things are of good report, if there is any virtue and if there is anything praiseworthy—meditate on these things."

- **2 Corinthians 5:17,** "Therefore, if anyone is in Christ, he is a new creation; old things have passed away; behold, all things have become new."

- **Colossians 3:10,** "And have put on the new man who is renewed in knowledge according to the image of Him who created him."

- **Hebrews 11:6,** "But without faith it is impossible to please Him, for he who comes to God must believe that He is, and that He is a rewarder of those who diligently seek Him."

Declaration for Your Mind

- Death and life are in the power of my tongue, so I speak life over my mind. I cast all my cares upon God because He cares for me. It is His will for me to be healed. He will keep me in perfect peace because my mind is stayed on Him. I confess that I will not be anxious, but in everything, by prayer and supplication with thanksgiving, I will let my request be made known to God, and the peace of God, which surpasses all understanding, will guard my heart and mind through Christ Jesus.

- I declare that I will not have an anxious mind because I have the mind of Christ. I desire to lead a quiet life, to mind my own business, and to work with my own hands.

- Lord, You have not given me a spirit of fear but of power, love, and a sound mind. I will love you, Lord my God, with all my heart, with all my soul, and with all my mind. I proclaim that I will not be conformed to this world but will be transformed by the renewing of my mind.

- I bind and cast out every spirit of anxiety, fear, worry, doubt, double-mindedness, hopelessness, and confusion, and I command them to leave me now in Jesus' name.

- I set my mind on things above, not on things on earth. I choose to cast down all arguments, theories, and reasonings and every proud or high thing that sets itself up against the true knowledge of God, and I lead every thought and purpose away captive into the obedience of Christ the Messiah, the Anointed One.

- Thank you, Father. I am a new creature; old things have passed away; behold, all things have become new. I declare that whatever things are true, whatever things are noble, whatever things are just, whatever things are pure, whatever things are lovely, whatever things are of good report, if there is any virtue, and if there is anything praiseworthy, I choose to meditate and ponder on these things. I decree all this in the mighty, most powerful Name of Jesus. Amen.

—— Section 4 ——

PRAYING FOR OTHERS

And the second is like it: 'You shall love your neighbor as yourself.' **Matthew 22:39**

PRAYING FOR FAMILY, FRIENDS, AND OTHER PEOPLE

Father, in the Name of Jesus, I thank you for family, friends, and acquaintances. I am grateful for the opportunity to pray for other people. *You command us to love our neighbour as we love ourselves.*

I ask You, Lord, to reveal Your love, Your healing power, and Your presence to Your people. I pray You revive **(mention the person's name)_____** for Your name's sake. Show Your mercy, Lord. Your Word states that mercy triumphs over judgment. Father, I ask that You remove any and all judgements in their lives that the accuser may be using against Your children. I ask for healing and deliverance, and Lord, would You show us all the things that may be hindering healing and deliverance? I cry out, "Deliver, **(mention the person's name)** _____, O Lord."

Heavenly Father, I join my faith in agreement with Your Word; whatsoever we bind on earth is bound in heaven, and whatsoever we loose on earth is loosed in heaven. Lord, I loose healing, I loose wholeness, I loose restoration, I loose deliverance, and I loose strength.

I bind the power of **(mention the illness or disease)** _____ and command it to go now. I command every organ, cell, tissue, system, and bone to function the way God intends. Every disruption in the body. Blood pressure, blood cells, electrolytes, muscle, chemical, or electromagnetic frequency. I call you back into divine alignment now, by the power in the Name of Jesus.

I speak to **(mention the illness or disease)** _____ and say you must bow now; there is a name that is higher than you, the Name of Jesus.

Lord, let **(mention the person's name)** _____ know

Your joy, according to Your Word, the joy of the Lord is our strength. And let the weak say, "I am strong." Lord, grant strength to the weak and weary.

I speak and release life to **(mention the person's name)** _____ body right now.

Based on my covenant with the blood of the Lamb, I declare victory over all diseases, sickness, and pain.

In Jesus Mighty Name. Amen.

Confess the Promises of God

Lord, I release your word over **(mention the person's name)** _____.

- I declare that you shall live and not die, and declare the works of the Lord **(Psalm 118:17)**.

- The Lord Your God has turned the curse (disease or sickness) into a blessing because He loves you **(Deuteronomy 11:9)**.
- With long life, He will satisfy you and show you His salvation **(Psalm 91:16)**.

- Your days shall be one hundred and twenty years **(Genesis 6:3)**.

- And the years of your life will be many **(Proverbs 4:10)**.

- No evil shall befall you, nor shall any plague come near your dwelling **(Psalm 91:10)**.

- The Lord shall preserve you and keep you alive. And you will be blessed on earth. You will not be delivered to the will of your enemies **(Psalm 41:2)**.

- He will bless your bread and water and will take sickness away from the midst of you **(Exodus 23:25)**.

- As your days so shall your strength be **(Deuteronomy 33:25)**.

- He sent His Word and, healed you, and delivered you from all your destruction **(Psalm 107:20)**.

- The spirit of a man will sustain him in sickness **(Proverbs 18:14)**.

- Strengthen the weak hands and make firm the feeble knees. Say to the fearful-hearted, be strong, do not fear! Behold, your God will come and save you **(Isaiah 35:3-4)**.

- Your healing shall spring forth speedily **(Isaiah 53:8)**.

- Seek Me (the Lord) and live **(Amos 5:4)**.

WORDS OF ENCOURAGEMENT

I admonish you to take the Word with diligence and consistency, just as you take your medicine every day. If you are lackadaisical (lazy) about sickness and diseases in your body, they will stay in your body. Regarding sickness and disease in your body, you must be radical and persistent; to stay in the word until that thing—in this case, that disease or sickness —leaves your body.

You must possess a righteous wrath, boldness, and consistency.

When you receive healing or a manifestation that healing has begun, take the word daily as your daily vitamin, your maintenance treatment to remain in health and wholeness. The Word of God is alive and full of power. If you have any doubts, then be encouraged by King David's words in **Psalms 138:2**.

> "I will worship toward at Your holy temple. And praise Your name. For Your loving-kindness and Your truth. For You have magnified Your word above all Your name."

Also, see **Isaiah 55:11** (AMPC):

> "So shall My word be that goes forth out of My mouth: it shall not return to Me void [without producing any effect, useless], but it shall accomplish that which I please and purpose, and it shall prosper in the thing for which I sent it."

I'm encouraging you to speak up for your healing and deliverance from sickness in this *pey* decade. We are in the Hebrew year of 5784, and in Hebrew, numbers have a pictorial meaning, and the word pey is pictured as a mouth, which is the number eighty (80). Hence the decade of the mouth.

Speak up and witness how it changes your life and health as you proclaim God's truth. Grab hold of any of the healing promises and make them a part of you. I am waiting to hear your testimonies. God did it for me. My prayer for you is, "Do it again, Lord! For anyone who would dare to put a demand and trust in Your Word. Your Word is life."

References

Andrew Wommac, Don't limit God
https://www.youtube.com/watch?v=Zx8uWrE-O7A&t=207s, 2024

Prophet Lovy Elias, 10 Reason You will be Healed, https://www.youtube.com/watch?v=kiP_YbTelvs, 2024

Dr Sharon Nesbitt, Divine Health; Frequency of Healing
https://www.youtube.com/watch?v=pz5OUUUHN9Y, 2024

https://www.google.com/search?q=mind+meaning&sca_esv=354005c37d90d315&sca_upv=1&rlz=1C1CHZN_enGB1053GB1053&sxsrf=ACQVn0__yXVldKTd0bu-j0SE0erGEygzKA%3A1712866614199&ei=NkUYZs7VC-qohbIPpKyasAk&ved=0ahUKEwjOyNiw_ 2024

https://www.google.com/search?q=declaration+meaning&sca_esv=354005c37d90d315&sca_upv=1&rlz=1C1CHZN_enGB1053GB1053&sxsrf=ACQVn080iDy_ 2024

https://www.google.com/search?q=whole+meaning&sca_esv=354005c37d90d315&sca_upv=1&rlz=1C1CHZN_enGB1053GB1053&sxsrf=ACQVn080iDy_ 2024

Dr D.K.Olukaya, Prayer Rain the Most Powerful and Practical Prayer Manual ever Written; Mountain of Fire and Miracles ministries (1999)

Suzette. T. Caldwell, Praying to Change your Life a Guide to Productive Prayer, Destiny image Publishers, INC (2009)